FAVORITE DOG BREEDS

SAINT BERNARDS

by Martha E. H. Rustad

I0893533

AMICUS HIGH INTEREST • AMICUS INK

Amicus High Interest and Amicus Ink are imprints of Amicus
P.O. Box 227, Mankato, MN 56002
www.amicuspublishing.us

Library of Congress Cataloging-in-Publication Data
Names: Rustad, Martha E. H. (Martha Elizabeth Hillman), 1975- author.
Title: Saint Bernards / by Martha E. H. Rustad.
Description: Mankato, Minnesota : Amicus, [2018] | Series: Favorite dog breeds | Audience: K to grade 3. | Includes index.
Identifiers: LCCN 2016036530 (print) | LCCN 2016046375 (ebook) | ISBN 9781681511306 (library binding) | ISBN 9781681521619 (pbk.) | ISBN 9781681512204 (ebook) | ISBN 9781681512204 (pdf)
Subjects: LCSH: Saint Bernard dog--Juvenile literature. | Dog breeds--Juvenile literature.
Classifica tion: LCC SF429.S3 R77 2018 (print) | LCC SF429.S3 (ebook) | DDC 636.73--dc23
LC record available at https://lccn.loc.gov/2016036530

Photo Credits: cynoclub cover; Charles Thatcher 4-5; Chronicle/Alamy Stock Photo 6-7; cynoclub 2, 9, 10-11, 14; Rita Kochmarjova 12-13, 18; Yoko Aziz/age fotostock 17; Roberto A Sanchez 20-21; GlobalP 22

Editor: Wendy Dieker
Designer: Tracy Myers
Photo Researcher: Holly Young

TABLE OF CONTENTS

NANNY DOG

A huge dog lies on the floor. A little girl comes over. She pulls its ears. She pats its nose. The big dog doesn't mind. It licks the girl. Saint Bernard dogs are huge and gentle.

Furry Fact

Saint Bernards are known as nanny dogs. They are gentle with kids.

6

MOUNTAIN DOGS

The Saint Bernard dog began in the **Swiss Alps**. These dogs helped **monks** rescue people stuck in the snow. They made paths in the deep snow. Today some still work as rescue dogs. They are also good pets.

BIG, BIG, BIG

A Saint Bernard is a big dog. It can weigh more than a grown person. Even sitting, it can be taller than a kid. It has a very large head and big, floppy ears.

Furry Fact

Saint Bernards need to learn not to jump up on people. They are so big! They could knock people down.

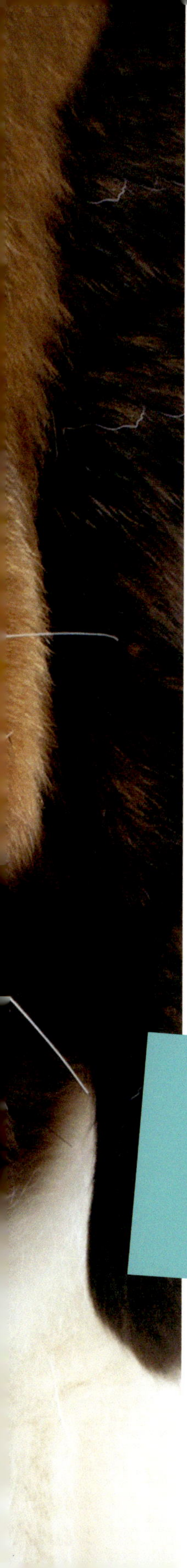

NOSE AND MOUTH

The nose of a Saint Bernard is wide. It has a strong sense of smell. Its big mouth has drooping lips. This dog drools a lot.

Furry Fact

A Saint Bernard doing rescue work can smell a person buried under snow.

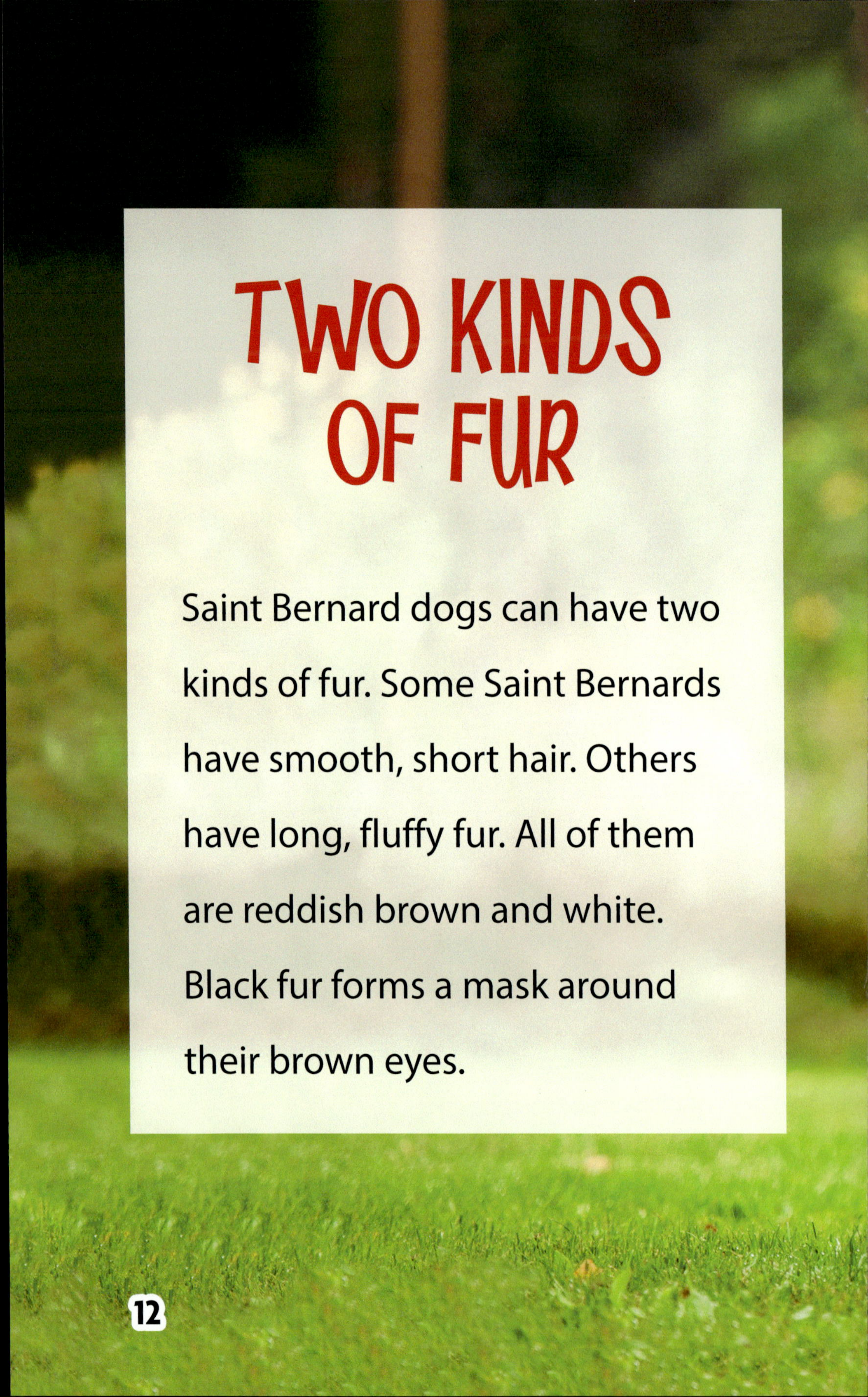

TWO KINDS OF FUR

Saint Bernard dogs can have two kinds of fur. Some Saint Bernards have smooth, short hair. Others have long, fluffy fur. All of them are reddish brown and white. Black fur forms a mask around their brown eyes.

TRAINING

Saint Bernard dogs are smart. They can quickly learn to obey. These giant dogs don't know their own strength. Owners **train** them to be calm and gentle.

STRONG DOGS

Saint Bernard dogs can learn to pull. Owners put a **harness** on the dog. It hooks to a cart. In snow, these strong dogs pull sleds. They can pull very heavy loads.

Furry Fact

Some Saint Bernards compete in pulling contests. They pull loads as heavy as a small car.

Metropole

PUPPIES

Six to ten puppies are born in a **litter**. They weigh only 1 or 2 pounds (0.5–1 kg). But they grow to be much bigger. In about two years, they are fully grown.

GENTLE GIANTS

Saint Bernard dogs are kind, smart, and lovable. They would rather not be alone. They like to be with their owners. These dogs are gentle giants.

HOW DO YOU KNOW IT'S A SAINT BERNARD?

WORDS TO KNOW

harness - straps that go around an animal's chest and body

litter - a group of puppies born at the same time

monk - a man who lives in a religious group and dedicates his life to God's work

Swiss Alps - a mountain range in Switzerland

train - to teach an animal how to behave

LEARN MORE

Books

Clapper, Nikki Bruno. *Saint Bernards.* Big Dogs. North Mankato, Minn: Capstone Press, 2016.

Rudolph, Jessica. *Saint Bernard: Mountain Rescuer.* Big Dogs Rule. New York: Bearport, 2012.

Websites

American Kennel Club: St. Bernard
http://www.akc.org/dog-breeds/st-bernard/

Dogs 101: Saint Bernard
http://www.animalplanet.com/tv-shows/dogs-101/videos/saint-bernard/

INDEX